be ... ... ranch of the
... ow...

D0296592

The Minaret Speaks

SAYYED ABUL HASAN 'ALI NADWI

UK ISLAMIC ACADEMY

© UK Islamic Academy, 2005

ISBN 1 872531 16 4

All rights reserved. No part of this publication may be reproduced, stored in a retrieval system or transmitted in any form or by any means, electronic, mechanical, photocopying, recording or otherwise, without the prior permission of the copyright owner.

General Editor: Iqbal Ahmad Azami

Published by
UK Islamic Academy
147 Mere Road
Leicester LE5 5GQ
United Kingdom

Website: www.ukiabooks.com
E-mail: info@ukiabooks.com

British Library Cataloguing in Publication Data
A catalogue record for this book is available from the British Library

Illustrations: M. Ishaq
Design and Typesetting: Sohail Nakhooda & Muhammad al-Madani

Introduction

In the name of Allah, the most gracious, the most merciful

Allah is the creator and sustainer of all things. Only Allah knew what was in store for the people of the East, among them millions of Muslims, who migrated from their own countries to the Western world. This included a large number of Muslims from the Indian subcontinent. Despite their parents' personal knowledge and experiences, Muslim children know very little about their Islamic roots in India.

Islam has a very rich history in India, having ruled it for hundreds of years. There are still famous Muslim scholars in all fields of knowledge and exploration throughout the world. There is a great need to have something for Muslim children, whose parents are from the Indian subcontinent, to be proud of, and to learn from their past history. For this we have selected an imaginary narrative of Islamic history in India written by Sayyed Abul Hasan Ali Nadwi, one of the most commanding Islamic historians of the subcontinent. He narrates the history of Islam as observed and related by the Minaret of Qutbuddin, a famous Islamic monument in Delhi, India.

We hope that children will find the story interesting, and that it will create among them an eagerness to know more about their parents' and ancestors' history and thereby strengthen their Islamic identity.

Allah is the First and the Last, and with His favour, all good deeds are accomplished.

Sha'ban 1426 AH
September 2005

Iqbal Ahmad Azami

3

I

One day I decided to have a break from the hubbub of the markets and the pressure of my work in the city of Delhi. I visited the minaret of Qutbuddin which lies outside the city.

As I gazed up at this lofty minaret, built from hard, red sandstone which is a marvel of architecture, I thought how perfect an example it was of the greatness of the Muslims in Delhi's past.

As I was walking around the minaret, amid the tombs and palaces, reflecting on the fragility of man and the strength of what he builds, I heard a voice say: 'O man! Listen!'

I turned round but I could not see anyone. I looked everywhere but the place was empty. No one was there except the deaf and dumb stones.

Then the voice repeated: 'O man! Listen!' I listened and went towards the minaret where I experienced a miracle – I heard the minaret speak.

'I have never heard a stone speak or a minaret talk until today!', I exclaimed.

Then the voice became louder and clearer: 'Listen, O man and do not be afraid! Allah, Who makes everyone speak, has made me speak.'

I listened intently to more of what this voice had to say. It went on: 'I have been standing here for seven centuries without moving so much as an eyelid. I have watched the ups and downs of time and the changing of kings and rulers as if I were the pivot around which the whole cycle of events revolves.

'During this time I have seen happy events which made me smile a little and sorrowful occasions which made me weep a lot. If my heart was not made of stone there were times when it would have broken from grief.

'I have also seen some good kings, and pious men who have delighted me and made me forget my frequent sorrows.

'I will tell you about some things I have heard and seen in this land.

'I heard that Sultan Mahmud, the Ghaznavid, opened up this land to Islam. He defeated all his enemies and routed the armies of the kings of India. His actions proved that faith can overcome force of numbers. That happened at the beginning of the fifth century AH/ eleventh century CE.

'One hundred and fifty years later Sultan Shihabuddin Ghauri invaded India. He gave Muslims security in this land and established an independent state for them.

'But the person who really created an Islamic state was Shaykh Mo'inuddin Chishti. He was able to guide thousands of idol-worshippers to Islam. His supplication was a weapon and shield for Ghauri.

'I say, "I heard", because I did not exist in those days. I am a child of the seventh century. Qutbuddin built me as the minaret for the Quwwatul-Islam mosque and his work was completed by Shamsuddin. I have remained alone since then.

'One of the beauties of Islam is that it can make slaves into kings. Ghauri was succeeded by his slave Qutbuddin who, in turn, was followed by his slave Shamsuddin. The Mamluk kingdom which lasted for eighty-seven years gave us splendid kings like General Qutbuddin Aybak, virtuous ones like Nasiruddin Mahmud ibn Altamash, and just ones like Ghayathuddin Balban.

'During the reign of Sultan Shamsuddin, there was a great shaykh in Delhi whose name was Qutbuddin Bakhtyar Ka'ki. I often saw Sultan Shamsuddin visit the Shaykh at night to serve him in complete humility.

'Then the kingdom of the Mamluk masters came to

an end. *The earth belongs to Allah and He bequeaths it to whomever He will.* The Khiljis came and I saw the monstrous deeds that man can commit. A noble uncle was killed by his nephew and son-in-law.

'But after 'Ala'uddin killed his uncle, Jalaluddin, he restored order to the land. He established laws, set just prices and brought security throughout India. He also conquered other parts of India to extend his empire. After thirty-one years the Khilji dynasty collapsed and was replaced by the Tughluqs who included King Muhammad Tughluq, a mad intellectual who wanted to move the capital of India to Dawlatabad. Allah was merciful to me in my loneliness and the king did not succeed.

'Muhammad Tughluq was followed by a righteous young man from his family called Firoz, who built mosques and schools. He also constructed streets and

hostels for visitors and put right many of the injustices experienced by the people at that time.

'During this period lived Shaykh Nizamuddin Badayuni. He had a flourishing *zawiyah* centre for Islamic learning and moral training, which attracted Muslims seeking spiritual solace. In Shaykh Nizam they found a humble scholar who commanded great respect. A spiritual emirate was able to exist within the materialistic state, and offered the people an alternative way of life.

'The Tughluq family's rule ended after 135 years. Afterwards the Lodhis came. Sikander Lodhi, the best known, was a just king who had a great thirst for knowledge and encouraged scholarship.

'During this time the city of Jawnpur flourished, reaching its peak during the reign of Ibrahim Shah Sharqi (804–44 AH/1402–36 CE). Jawnpur was situated between the Sultanates of Delhi and Bengal. I listened to the tales of its kings and the accounts of such scholars as Qadi Shihabuddin Dawlatabadi and Shaykh 'Abul-Fath ibn 'Abdul-Muqtadir Dihlawi. What rich stories were told of their mosques and schools.

'The city of Ahmadabad founded by Ahmad Shah also flourished. It excelled the other parts of India under the influence of its kind and upright kings and renowned *hadith* scholars. Their guidance was reflected in the disciplined society of the times. The Islamic way of life was also apparent in the crafts and gardens. When I heard news of Mahmud Shah and his son Muzaffar Shah al-Halim (862–932 AH/1456–1526 CE) it was as if I was listening once again to reports of the first generation of Muslims, who were the very cream of the history of mankind.

'At this time the spiritual and moral links with the rest of the Muslim world were strengthened. India rightly reflected the culture and faith of Islam. The remains of countless buildings from this time can still be seen in and around Delhi. Mosques, forts and tombs illustrate the Muslim rulers' interest in architecture as an art form to glorify the Magnificence of Allah.'

II

'In 933 AH/1526 CE, when the Lodhi king Ibrahim was ruling here, Babar, a Timur, arrived from Kabul which he had already occupied before attacking India. He routed the Lodhi armies, who numbered 100,000 fighters, on the plain of Panipat with a mere 12,000 men. It was yet another proof that determination can overcome numbers. Babar established the Mughal government and this sent vibrations all over the world and had a lasting effect on India.

'During the reign of Babar's son, Humayun, Sher Shah Suri rose up and expelled Humayun to Persia. Sher Shah took control of Delhi and during a magnificent reign proved to be a great administrator. He was also devoted to scholarly pursuits. He built mosques, forts and tombs and is also well remembered for his road building.

'He provided trees, mosques, wells and hostels at regular intervals along the new roads for the benefit of travellers. All this was accomplished in a mere five years. The successors of Sher Shah were weak and Humayun, after fifteen years in exile, managed to regain his throne with the help of the Shah of Persia.

'Humayun was succeeded by his eldest and near-illiterate son, Akbar, who reigned for fifty years. Akbar abandoned Islam and tried

to establish a new religion. He was a great disappointment to the Muslims. Allah helped to protect me from his foolish ideas when Akbar made Agra his capital instead of Delhi.

'Akbar was followed by Jahangir who was a much better ruler than his father. He managed to eradicate many of the evil influences that held sway during his father's reign.

'During this time a great reformer, Shaykh Ahmad Sirhindi al-Mujaddid (d.1034 AH/1624 CE) appeared on the scene. His inspirational teaching brought Islam back into the lives of the people. He encouraged them to shun the evil practices that were popular under Akbar.

'At this time India was also well served by the great scholar 'Abdul-Haq Bukhari. He specialised in the science of *hadith*. I am happy that he studied in rooms near to me and, since he is buried here, he stays close by.

'Jahangir was followed by his son, Shah Jahan, who was responsible for constructing many magnificent monuments in India. In Delhi, he built the Jame' Masjid in red sandstone and white marble. It is one of the most beautiful mosques in the world. He also built the Red Fort, named after its outer sandstone walls, which took nine years to complete.

'Shah Jahan laid the foundation stone for the Red Fort a year after he transferred his capital from Agra to Delhi. He also built the famous Taj Mahal over the grave of his wife. It is an exquisite monument of white marble, resting on red sandstone. The only reason I can think of for leaving my present site would be to see it.

'Shah Jahan was imprisoned by his son, Aurangzeb 'Alamgir, who then took the throne and reigned for fifty years. He attacked the lax ways into which Muslims had strayed. He appointed great and learned scholars to compile a standard work on Islamic Law. All the judgements, the rulings of previous jurists were gathered under the direct supervision and sound guidance of Emperor Aurangzeb and when completed became known as *Fatawa Alamgiri*. This is a magnificent collection in many volumes. It is a vast record of Islamic rulings and judgements, and is a work of reference still used by lawyers. To scholars it is a greater monument of learning than all the architectural monuments of the Mughal period in India.

'Aurangzeb abolished taxes and removed many injustices from the long-suffering Muslims. He also imposed the *jizyah*; a tax levied on the unbelievers in the state and set up *muhtasibs* to safeguard standards of behaviour. He established a state where knowledge and *din* were paramount.

'Sadly, his successors were men of weak faith. Politics became a mockery and the state a plaything. Kings ruling in the morning would be murdered by evening. They changed like people change their clothes. I will not waste your time by mentioning the names of these people.

'What I saw made me weep bitterly. The morals of the Muslims were so corrupt at this time that alcoholic drinks were widespread, musical instruments were commonplace and people indulged in such amusements as singing and dancing. It was as if no Prophet had ever been sent, and no Book sent down. The people were living in a state of ignorance.

'I remembered the words of Allah the Almighty, *"When we decide to destroy a population, We (first) send a definite order among them who are given the good things of this life and yet transgress; so that the word is proven true against them, then We destroy them utterly"* (17: 16) and I feared His punishment.

'In the time of Muhammad Shah Rangila matters came to a head. The emperor of Persia, Nadir Shah, came in 1151 AH/1738 CE and put the population to the sword. In Delhi alone 150,000 were killed and the streets flowed with blood. The killing continued for three days.

'The Muslims' behaviour still did not improve and they were so weak that the Marathas and Sikhs joined

forces against them to attack, plunder and pillage. Many towns were destroyed and mosques, where the name of Allah was mentioned, were demolished. The Muslims were powerless to resist, and cowardice and fear overcame them.

'Then Allah was merciful to this Indian community and sent to it Ahmad Shah Abdali from Afghanistan in 1174 AH/1760 CE. He clashed with the Marathas on the battlefield at Panipat, killing 200,000 of them. He inflicted on them a devastating defeat from which they never recovered.

'In those barren days Delhi gave birth to a great man, Shah Waliyyullah ibn 'Abdur-Rahim. He re-called

Muslims to the true Islamic way of life and criticised the tyrannical rulers and false religious leaders who had allowed the people to go astray. He trained rightly-guided scholars and wrote marvellous books to share his knowledge of Islam.

'He and his three highly-respected sons, Shah 'Abdul-'Aziz, Shah Rafi'uddin and Shah 'Abdul-Qadir and his grandson Shah Muhammad Isma'il (buried at Balakot) translated the Qur'an, wrote detailed explanations on the *hadith* and *fiqh* and purified the people's hearts. They spent their lives explaining the *hadith*, teaching about *jihad* and martyrdom in the way of Allah, and about the Next World. Under their guidance I saw India flourish again.'

III

'Now I want to tell you of my saddest moments. The British came to India 400 years ago. They founded a trading company called the East India Company which took advantage of the local people. Unfortunately, the Muslim kings ignored the warning signs and co-operated with the unbelievers.

'The East India Company continued to trade with us and eventually the Mughal government were weakened enough to be intimidated. Then the officers of the company started to interfere in affairs of state. They sowed the seeds of discord between the *amirs* and incited them to oppose one another. They seized one opportunity after another until they became a powerful force in India.

'British trade and influence continued to get stronger and always at the expense of the Indians whose position grew steadily weaker. The British took Karnatak in the south and Calcutta in the east without any of their own blood being spilled.

'At last the young Nawab Sirajuddawla, the *Amir* of Murshidabad, decided to take action against the British who were draining India of its wealth. He marched with a great army from Murshidabad to Fort William and took prisoner 145 people who worked for a British company.

'In retaliation, the British army attacked the Muslims at the village of Plassey in 1171 AH/1757 CE. One of Sirajuddawla's ministers, Mir Ja'far, turned traitor and deserted to the British side and because of this Sirajuddawla was defeated. As a result, part of Bengal was lost to the British and Mir Ja'far became their governor, replacing the *Amir*.

'In a second attempt to oust the British, Mir Qasim, Shah 'Alam King of Delhi and the Nawab Shuja'ud-

dawla, the *Amir* of Oudh, joined forces. They fought the British at the Battle of Baksar in 1178 AH/1764 CE. The British though fewer in number, were better organised and the Indians were defeated once again. The British were now masters of Bengal, the richest province in India.

'Then a zealous, proud youth came on the scene. He became Sultan Tipu, the *Amir* of Mysore and the most powerful ruler in Southern India. He fought the British in a fierce battle in 1214 AH/1799 CE but was defeated. The British governor had taken 4000 troops from Britain to India and he besieged Sultan Tipu's capital, Seringapatam. He stormed the city with a force of 5000 which included Muslims and Marathas.

'This time one of Sultan Tipu's ministers, Mir Sadiq, betrayed the Sultan and deserted to the British. The Sultan died a hero defending his *din* and homeland.

'Allah wanted to test the people of India, so He gave them another opportunity to regain their Islamic way of life. A group of sincere youths, led by Sayyed Ahmad, a young man descended from the Messenger of Allah, peace and blessings be upon him, arrived from the East. I remember often seeing Sayyed Ahmad in the *madrasah* of Shah 'Abdul-'Aziz, and in the mosque of Shah 'Abdul-Qadir.

'Sayyed Ahmad attracted people from a wide area. He was supported by Shah Muhammad Isma'il, the nephew of Shah 'Abdul-'Aziz, Shaykh 'Abdul-Hayy, a great scholar of Delhi and the son-in-law of Shah 'Abdul-'Aziz, and many other righteous men.

'They visited towns and villages, trying all the while to bring people back to Islam. They ignited the flame of *jihad* in the people. They gathered around them the best of men who were known for their *din*, their worship of Allah, their good character and their enthusiasm.

'In 1241 AH/1825 CE these men, with strong Muslim support went to the Indian frontier and raised the banner of *jihad* against the Sikhs. A war broke out between the Muslims and the Sikhs and a short time later I heard that the Muslims had captured land and set up an emirate based on the Caliphate of the Rightly-Guided Caliphs.

'They implemented the laws of the *Shari'ah*, established prayer, paid *zakat*, commended the right and forbade the wrong. They conquered Peshawar, the frontier capital and became established. They intended to establish a legal independent state in India and corresponded with other *amirs* including the *Amir* of Bukhara and Chitral and the *amirs* of Afghanistan.

'Although the Muslims seemed happy, I was afraid that they would be victims of treachery and betrayal. My apprehension was well justified as only a few days later, I heard that the Afghani *amirs* had betrayed these good men and killed their nawab and their governors and that they were now on their way to Kashmir.

'Some days later I heard that they had been attacked in the remote valley of Balakot in the mountains of Hazara. Most of those noble men were killed in this painful event of 1246 AH/1831 CE.

'Another precious opportunity had been lost. *Only Allah can command what occurs.*

'Now I will return to the story of the British in India. They invaded the Punjab, Sind, Burma and Oudh and captured them all.

'However the Indians rose up to free themselves from the British in 1273 AH/1857 CE.

'The great rebellion shook the British to the core and it took them fourteen months to regain control. The revolt failed due to the Indians being poorly organised and the strong position of the British at the time. They punished the Indians mercilessly and took painful retribution from them. They overthrew the Mughal dynasty which had lasted for almost 350 years and the last Mughal emperor, Bahadur Shah, was exiled to Rangoon.

'From that day Indian Muslims were disheartened. They became weak in both religion and worldly affairs. Food supplies were erratic and prices increased. Famines

became commonplace, schools failed to provide proper education, *zawiyahs* were closed and mosques deserted.

'In 1366 AH/1947 CE, India was liberated from the British. Terrible riots in the last decade before the liberation caused many Muslims to emigrate from their homelands to establish a Muslim nation in north-western India. Others, in a state of despair, stayed around me to live under the non-Muslim government.

'I do not despair from the mercy of Allah as *"only those who err despair from His mercy."* I do not despair; I believe that the Muslims will rise again. I have seen them. They are like the sun which sets in one place on the horizon, yet, rises from another. They are like the stars. If one star disappears, another one rises. Muslims can re-emerge in their former glory in just the same way. The righteous future of the world is in their hands and *"Allah does not love corruption in the earth, nor is He pleased with disbelief"*.

'Greet your community from me and say to it that I testify to Allah that this community has prospered only when holding to its *din* and has lost when being heedless of that *din*. This community will only be put right by what put its first days right. This is what I have seen and experienced throughout these long centuries.'

When the minaret had finished speaking, I left it and returned home. I spent the night reflecting on what I had heard. The next day I wrote down this account of India's history as told to me by that lofty minaret. 🙠

Glossary

Amir: a leader or ruler, a term generally used for provincial/regional rulers.

Din: religion, the Islamic way of life.

Fatawa: plural of *Fatwa*, religious opinions or rulings of jurists.

Fatawa-'Alamgiri: a great encyclopaedic book in which rulings of previous jurists according to the Hanafi School are compiled. The work was done under the direct supervision and participation of the Mogul emperor of India, Aurangzeb 'Alamgir; it therefore became known as *Fatawa-'Alamgiri*.

Fiqh: deep understanding of Islam. Islamic jurisprudence.

Hadith: traditions of the Prophet, may Allah bless him and grant him peace, sayings, deeds and silent approvals, which means something was done in his presence or came to his knowledge and he did not oppose it.

Jihad: to struggle in the way of Allah. To serve the Islamic cause which includes fighting in the way of Allah against His enemies, as and when necessary.

Jizyah: a tax levied on non-Muslim subjects of an Islamic state, against the responsibility of guarding their lives, honour and property. It should be noted that Muslims pay *Zakah* on their property and every able Muslim is subject to be called up for army service whenever the need arises, from which non-Muslims are exempt in an Islamic state.

Madrasah: place of learning, an Islamic school.

Muhtasib: inspectors, particularly officers known for their honesty and piety, appointed by the government to check and inspect the behaviour of officers in the government offices.

Nawab: rulers of regional provinces, subject to the central empire but independent in their regions.

Qadi: a jurist, justice for an Islamic court.

Rangila: Muhammad Shah, one of the Mogul emperors who was known for his extravagance and his love of dancing and drinking, and became known as Rangila the funny.

Shah: King. It is also used as a title for a respected, knowledgeable person, such as Shah Waliyyullah and Shah 'Abdul 'Aziz Dehlawi.

Shari'ah: Islamic law.

Shaykh: a respected person, a pious and spiritual leader or a very knowledgeable person. It is also used as a title for present-day Gulf rulers.

Zawiyah: a corner, or exclusive place of worship, for remembrance of Allah, and a centre for spiritual training.